BACKYARD

That's Gross!
A Look at Science

Julie Murray

Big Buddy BOOKS
That's Gross!

VISIT US AT
www.abdopublishing.com

Published by ABDO Publishing Company, 8000 West 78th Street, Edina, Minnesota 55439.

Copyright © 2009 by Abdo Consulting Group, Inc. International copyrights reserved in all countries. No part of this book may be reproduced in any form without written permission from the publisher. Buddy Books™ is a trademark and logo of ABDO Publishing Company.

Printed in the United States.

Coordinating Series Editor: Rochelle Baltzer
Editor: Sarah Tieck
Contributing Editor: Marcia Zappa
Graphic Design: Deborah Coldiron
Cover Photograph: *iStockPhoto:* iStockPhoto, Michal Rozanski; *Photos.com:* Jupiter Images.
Interior Photographs/Illustrations: *AP Photo:* Rich Pedroncelli (p. 15); *iStockPhoto:* Denis Ananiadis (p. 25), Christopher Badzioch (p. 27), Denice Breaux (p. 23), Jani Bryson (pp. 16, 18, 24), Christian Carroll (p. 29), Jacek Chabraszewski (p. 10), Gordon Dixon (p. 23), Merrill Dyck (p. 20), David Hernandez (p. 30), Emma Holmwood (p. 11), iStockPhoto (pp. 5, 8), Cat London (p. 28), Stacey Newman (pp. 7, 30), Michal Rozanski (p. 23), William Sherman (p. 11), Mike Sonnenberg (pp. 9, 14, 26), Chad Truemper (p. 17); *Peter Arnold, Inc:* James Gerholdt (p.19), Philippe Hays (p. 21), Hans Pfletschinger (p. 27), Tom Vezol (p. 9), Wildlife (p. 13); *Photos.com:* Jupiter Images (pp. 5, 7, 29).

Library of Congress Cataloging-in-Publication Data

Murray, Julie, 1969-
  Backyard / Julie Murray.
    p. cm. -- (That's gross! A look at science)
  ISBN 978-1-60453-553-2
  1. Urban animals--Juvenile literature. I. Title.

QL49.M883 2009
591.75'6--dc22

                             2008036380

Contents

Exploring the Backyard

Your backyard is amazing! People play. Gardens grow. And, sun shines. Look a little closer. You'll see that behind all that cool stuff is a lot of yuck. Some of it is natural. Some of it is unhealthy. Let's explore!

What's That Smell?

Did you know that animal poop helps gardens grow? Poop from animals is called manure (muh-NUR).

Manure acts as a **fertilizer** (FUHR-tuh-leye-zuhr). It adds **nutrients** (NOO-tree-uhnts) to the soil. And, it helps soil take in and hold water.

Farmers use manure for their crops, too!

Many times, gardeners mix manure with grass clippings or hay. They wait for months before using it so the mixture can age. This is called "cooking the pile."

Scoop that poop!

Don't leave pet poo all over your yard as fertilizer. Dog and cat poop can make people sick. Gardeners mostly use manure from cows, horses, and chickens.

Hiding Under Rocks

Lots of creepy, crawly creatures live in backyards! But, one of the yuckiest is called a centipede (SEHN-tuh-peed).

Centipedes have lots of legs. During the day, these scary buggers hide out in dark, **damp** places. They're found under wooden boards, rocks, and leaf piles. They come out to hunt at night.

A centipede's body has many parts called segments. Most centipedes have one pair of legs on each segment, except the rear. All of those legs help centipedes move very quickly!

Millipedes are a lot like centipedes. But, they look more like worms. And, they have two pairs of legs on most of their body segments.

For real?

The world's largest centipede is the Amazonian giant centipede. It grows to be about 11 inches (28 cm) long. Scientists say it can catch flying bats and eat them! It can also eat lizards, frogs, and birds!

Cute, but Gross

Rabbits sure are cute. But, they have a habit that is not so cute. They eat a special kind of poop called a cecotrope (SEE-koh-trohp).

When a rabbit eats grass or twigs, its body has a hard time taking in the **nutrients**. Some of the **digested** food is still useful. It comes out as a cecotrope.

Rabbits eat their own warm, fresh cecotropes as they come out. This helps them stay healthy!

Rabbits love to hang out in yards and gardens. But, most gardeners don't like them. Rabbits can eat plants very quickly!

Regular rabbit poop is hard and round. The tiny balls make good fertilizer for gardens.

11

Beneath the Grass

Have you ever dug into the ground and found gooey, white worms? These are June beetle larvae (LAHR-vee) known as white grubs.

Grubs live in soil. There, they feed on plant roots. This causes dead spots in yards. So, most gardeners consider them pests.

Grubs love to eat. This helps them grow into strong adult beetles.

What's Rotting?

Most gardens smell good. But if a garden has corpse flowers, it smells far from good. When corpse flowers bloom, they smell worse than garbage!

These huge, stinky flowers come from Indonesia. They bloom only once every few years. The flower smells like rotting meat. So, not many gardeners grow this plant.

Corpse flowers can be ten feet (3 m) tall! Some say their deep red color looks like raw meat.

Slithering Snakes

Snakes slide and hide in backyards. They are neat creatures. But, they are also very gross!

A snake's skin is cool and dry to touch. When the skin gets old, the snake grows new skin and crawls out of the old. This is called molting. The old skin is left behind in a pile.

Garter snakes commonly live in backyards. But don't worry! These small, striped snakes are not poisonous.

17

Some snakes have sharp, curved **fangs**. When they bite, poison comes out through their fangs. Some snakebites can kill a person. Others make skin swell and ooze blood.

But, most snakes don't bite people. They'd rather eat small animals, such as mice. A snake's jawbones are connected with **stretchy** skin. A snake can spread its jaw wide to swallow a mouse without chewing!

Yikes!

Rattlesnakes are poisonous. They make a loud rattling noise with their tail. This warns people to stay away.

Squirmy Worms

Too weird!
Earthworms have five hearts! And, they have a body part called a gizzard. This muscle uses small stones the worm has swallowed to grind up its food.

Earthworms live under the grass. Their bodies are long and slimy. A coating of **mucus** (MYOO-kuhs) covers their skin. Earthworms move through dirt, digging trails and turning soil. This work keeps backyards healthy.

Sometimes, earthworms come out of the ground when it rains. If they are in the sun too long, their bodies dry up. Yuck!

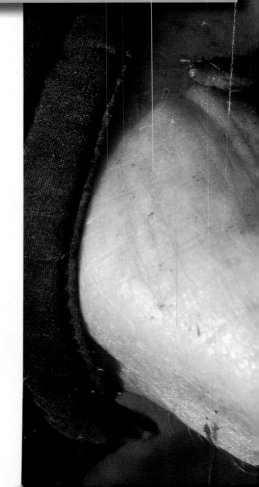

Many people believe that cutting a worm in half makes two worms. This isn't true. But if a worm is cut behind the body part that makes mucus, the front half can survive!

Some worms do a cool thing called composting. Composting turns garbage and waste into a natural **fertilizer** called compost. Compost is rich with **nutrients**. It helps plants grow.

To make compost, many people put red worms in piles or bins in their backyards. They bring yard waste and food garbage to the worms. The worms eat it and create **castings**. The castings pile up and turn into compost.

Red worms can eat their own weight in food every day!

Not all leftovers make good food for red worms. They mostly eat fruits and vegetables.

Dig In!

Lots of wild animals visit backyards. They leave behind poop, or dung. A bug called a dung beetle searches yards for the best pieces. Then, it rolls the dung into a ball. A single ball can be as big as an apple!

Dung beetles have many uses for the poo. Sometimes they eat it. Other times they lay their eggs in it and bury it in the ground.

Dung beetles do important work. By removing animal poop, they help keep yards healthy.

Bloodsuckers

Mosquitoes (muh-SKEE-tohs) eat dinner in backyards every night. One of their favorite meals is human blood.

Only female mosquitoes bite. They have a long, tubelike body part called a proboscis (pruh-BAH-suhs). It helps them make a hole in the skin. It also helps them suck out blood.

Most mosquito bites leave a red, itchy spot on skin. But, sometimes mosquito bites give people sicknesses.

Mosquito is a Spanish word that means "little fly."

Most mosquitoes lay eggs in standing water. Some eggs are in a group called a floating raft.

27

That WAS Gross!

Between stinky flowers, animal poo, and slimy worms, some very yucky things are in your backyard!

Now that you know about all the grossness, take a closer look. Many gross things are just a part of life and no big deal. Others can be prevented. Do what you can to live in a healthy way!

Get rid of standing water. This helps keep mosquitoes from laying eggs in your yard.

Clean up your pet's poop. If left outside, it can make your backyard an unhealthy place!

Overwatering the grass can lead to the growth of mushrooms. Some mushrooms are poisonous. So don't eat them!

Eeeeww! What is THAT?

Answer on page 32.

30

Important Words

casting something cast out, such as a worm's body waste.

damp having a small amount of wetness.

digest to break down food into parts small enough for the body to use.

fangs long, sharp teeth.

fertilizer something used to help plants grow.

mucus thick, slippery, protective fluid from the body.

nutrient something found in food that living beings take in for growth and development.

stretchy able to spread out to full size or greater.

Web Sites

To learn more about gross stuff, visit ABDO Publishing Company online. Web sites about gross stuff are featured on our Book Links page. These links are routinely monitored and updated to provide the most current information available.

www.abdopublishing.com

Index

"Eeeeww! What is THAT?" answer: a manure pile.